THE INSTRUMENT
OF
CARAVAGGIO

ANTONINO SAGGIO
ENGLISH TRANSLATION BY REBECCA GUARDA

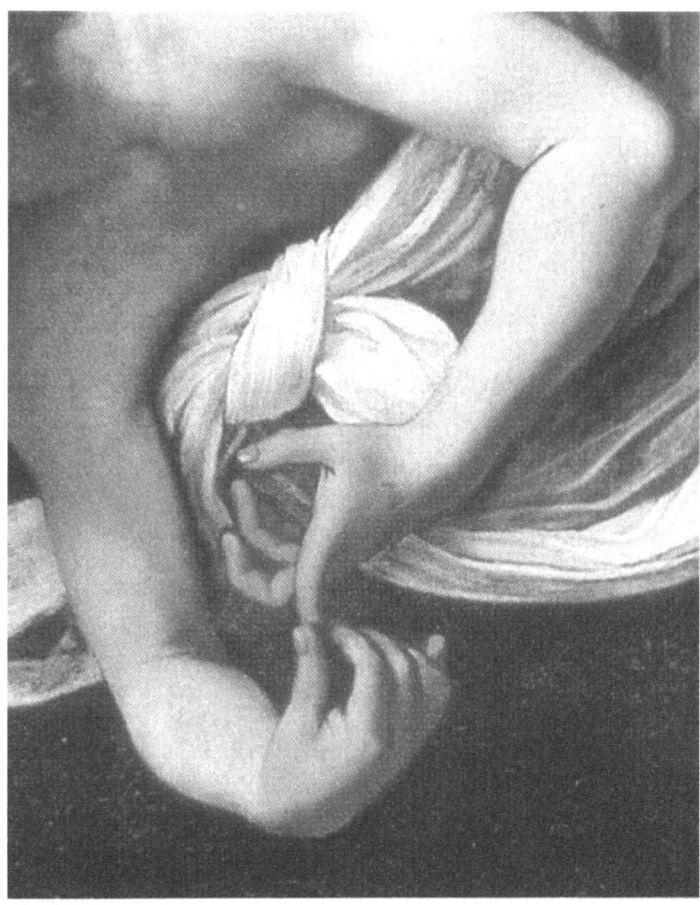

4 Lena

Milena di Nino
Maddalena di Michelangelo
Maria con il bambino
Madonna di tutti i pellegrini dello spirito

Published in October 2010 by Lulu.com in
Raleigh NC, USA
ISBN: 978-1-4461-2228-0

First English Edition.

First Edition in Italian Lulu.com and Kappa Roma,
Febbraio 2007
Lo Strumento di Caravaggio

Translated from Italian
by Architect Rebecca Guarda
www.rebeccaguarda.com/

Books by the this Author:

L'opera di Giuseppe Pagano tra politica e architettura (De-
dalo 1984)
Louis Sauer un architetto americano (Officina, 1988)
Using Goals in Design (Cmu, 1988)
Giuseppe Terragni vita e opere (Laterza, 1995, 2004, 2005)
Peter Eisenman trivellazioni nel futuro (Testo&Immagine
1996)
Frank Gehry architetture residuali (Testo&Immagine 1997)
*Introduzione alla rivoluzione informatica in architettura, The
IT Reolution in Architecture. Thoughts on a Paradigm Shift*
(Carocci 2007)
*Architettura e modernità dal Bauhaus alla rivoluzione Infor-
matica* (Carocci 2010)
Five Masterworks by Louis Sauer (Lulu.com 2010)

INDEX

The Instrument of Caravaggio

7 *The Break from the Frame*

8 *Proscenium*

13 *From Below*

19 *Flash*

21 *The Mirror*

22 *Camera Obscura*

23 *Ask the dust*

24 *Facts and deductions on the use of Caravaggio's instruments*

30 *Narcissus in time*

35 *Endnotes*

IMAGES

Unless otherwise noted, the artist is Michelangelo Merisi da Caravaggio.

.

p.

0 "Narcissus", (1600) 110 cm × 92 cm (43 in × 36 in), Galleria d'Arte Antica, Rome.

1 "Saint Matthew and the Angel", (1602) 295 cm × 195 cm (116 in × 77 in), Church of San Luigi dei Francesi, Contarelli Chapel, Rome detail.

6 "Death of the Virgin", (1605-1606) 369 cm × 245 cm (145 in × 96 in),, Louvre Museum, Paris,detail.

9 "The Calling of Saint Matthew", (1599-1600) 322 cm × 340 cm (127 in × 130 in), Church of San Luigi dei Francesi, Contarelli Chapel, Rome.

10 Ibidem detail.

10 "Basket of Fruit", (1595-1596) 31 cm × 47 cm (12 in × 19 in) Pinacoteca Ambrosiana, Milano.

11 "Cruxifiction of Saint Peter", (1600-1601) 230 cm × 175 cm (91 in × 69 in), Church of Santa Maria del Popolo, Cerasi Chapel, Rome.

12 "Death of the Virgin", (1605-1606) 369 cm × 245 cm (145 in × 96 in), Louvre Museum, Paris.

16 "Building Section of Sant'Ivo alla Sapienza by Francesco Borromini", (1632-1660) Rome. Renovation by Paolo Portoghesi.

17 "Madonna di Loreto or Madonna dei Pellegrini", (1603-1606), 260 cm × 150 cm (100 in × 59 in), Church of Sant'Agostino, Cavalletti Chapel, Rome.

18 "The Conversion of Saint Paul (or Conversion of Saul)", (1600-1601) 237 cm × 189 cm (93 in × 74 in), Church of Santa Maria del Popolo, Cerasi Chapel, Rome.

20 "Martha and Mary Magdalene" (1597) 100 cm × 134.5 cm (39 in × 53.0 in), Detroit Institute of Arts, Detroit, detail.

23 "Jupiter, Neptune and Pluto", (1597) 300 cm × 180 cm (120 in × 71 in), Casino of the Villa Ludovisi, Rome.

26 "John the Baptist (Reclining Baptist)" (1610) 106 cm × 179.5 cm (42 in × 70.7 in), Private Collection, Monaco di Baviera.

26 "Saint Jerome Writing" (1606) 112 cm × 157 cm (44 in × 62 in), Galleria Borghese, Rome.

27 "Mary Magdalen in Ecstasy", (1596) 106x91, Private collection, Rome.

29 "Boy with a Basket of Fruit or Young Self-Portrait", (1593) 70 cm × 67 cm (28 in × 26 in), Galleria Borghese,Rome detail.

29 "Bacchino Malato", (1592-1593) 67 cm × 53 cm (26 in × 21 in), Galleria Borghese, Rome detail.

31 "The Raising of Lazarus", (1608-1609) 380 cm × 275 cm (150 in × 108 in), Museo Regionale, Messina.

THE INSTRUMENT OF CARAVAGGIO

> Thus he came to his own empirical experience with the 'camera obscura', and this was nearly a scientific discovery – in any case his personal experience". What is most surprising is that this occurred at the times of Della Porta and, eventually, of Galileo.[1]

Paul Valéry states, with the words of Socrates, than in nature there is no difference between an action and the way in which it develops itself: "Such that to the same substance belongs the path taken, as the subject on the path and the time employed to run its course. If a man waves his arm he initiates a possible relationship. But, from the point of view of nature, the movement of the arm and the gesture itself cannot be separated".[2]

This image is the best one that I know of to illustrate the artistic practice of Caravaggio through his instrument.

If the gesture of the arm and the arm itself "cannot be separated" as Socrates-Valéry state then, the use of an instrument becomes in some way inseparable from the same movement. Instrument and representation, history and thought combined inextricably; influencing each other and interlaced with one another.

One thing is having at one's disposal the proven instrument already refined from generations of experimenters and artists. How a vision evolves in regards to the birth of "new" instruments is a completely different case. From the point of view of artistic expression, the introduction of an instrument is first of all "a crisis". It is often a great crisis (recent examples being photography, film, audio, the electronic calculator) and only after great efforts and upheavals or authentic revolutions in thought and of action, does it manage to reach a form of expression.

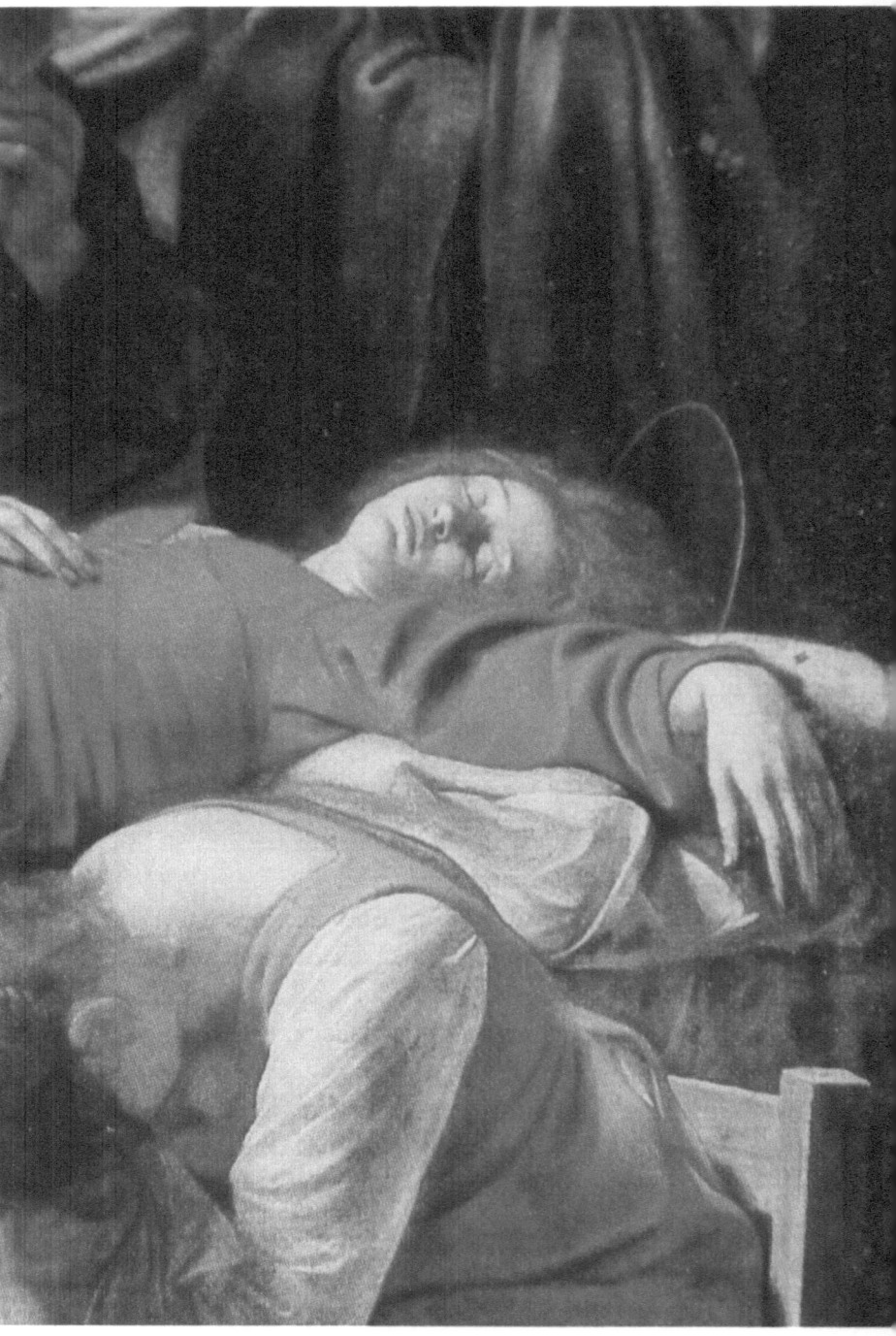

"Modernism… makes value of out of the crisis, and provokes an aesthetic breach",[3] This is the point. Caravaggio enables a new aesthetic to be born, an aesthetic that literally overturns the high to low, the rhetorical is simplified, perspective is proximity, the light is in the lightning bolt, static is in the dynamic, equilibrium is forever on edge. Covering some of the topics of Caravaggio's paintings together with the instrument determines a narrow visual angle. I believe, it is through the artifice of this very narrow gap that, the great light of the painting of Michelangelo Merisi will emerge.

The Break from the Frame

The world of Brunelleschi or Paolo Uccello or Antonello da Messina or of Dürer is to be seen through the perspective frame. The eye is fixed and dominates, the vanishing points converge, and there are no deviations or anomalies. The instrument (the perspective frame) and the mental construction (perspective) together with all the newest ways of thinking of man in the world, are enveloped one with the other like the arm and its very gesture. The window is the key of representation. The image is seen through a picture frame that frames the view and creates depth; and depth is realized through a gridded space, measured and governed from the laws of perspective. Caravaggio, on the contrary, closes the window dramatically and compresses space in order to explode it beyond the painting. 4 It is as if with Caravaggio the glass on which the regulating grid of perspectival space is placed has been shattered.

Let us look at the celebrated painting "The Calling of Matthew" in the Contarelli Chapel of the Church of San Luigi dei Francesi. The characters are compressed in a few tens of centimeters and are perspectivally behind the viewer. There exists no depth. The window in the picture is there, but it is purposefully closed, silent, mournful (and always sealed up as will be few windows Caravaggio paints). The space is finite; deep airy and perspectival. The many tens of meters in which we grasp a Piero della Francesca, or Antonello's space expanded far away to the horizon, become in contrast closed and compressed. It is this newer and intermediate space that takes place. The former spatial depth of perspective framed "within" the picture, is replaced by a new spatiality evoked "outside" of the picture frame into the space of the living.

This is further illustrated in his "Basket of Fruit" of 1597-1598 at the Ambrosiana of Milan. All is revealed here in the few centimeters of the composition's depth of fruit leaning on an axis against the wall. The basket projects "beyond" the axis and casts its own shadow on its support. The perspective vision is not only eliminated and its depth compressed to a minimum. The objects are literally in a precarious balance: in the balance between inside and outside, always ready to tumble as the only certain trace of their existence. This being in precarious balance is a fundamental key to understanding Caravaggio's revolution. It was as equally spatial as anti-perspectival. It is also much much more.

Proscenium

One could argue that this space in precarious equilibrium is compatible for a still life of fruit, but does not work in paintings that bring to life personages depicted in action. Exactly the contrary is true. The exact same type of space is asserted in nearly all of Caravaggio's paintings. Let us examine the "real" [5] still life, (the "Death of the Virgin" of 1604 for Santa Maria della Scala, but rejected by the Carmeliani di Trastevere and today exhibited in the Louvre). The idea of the inhabited picture frame, in this case, is represented physically with a curtain. This curtain encloses, unifies and compresses a new kind of space and immediately reveals that the inhabited frame is precisely a proscenium. The characters are not placed within the scene, but pointed directly on the proscenium; often extending literally beyond the frame and thereby putting themselves beside the viewer.

The proscenium is surely an "inhabited frame", but it is also much more. Its being in this precarious balance between inside and outside is not only a dry play of perception, but it is life itself that is

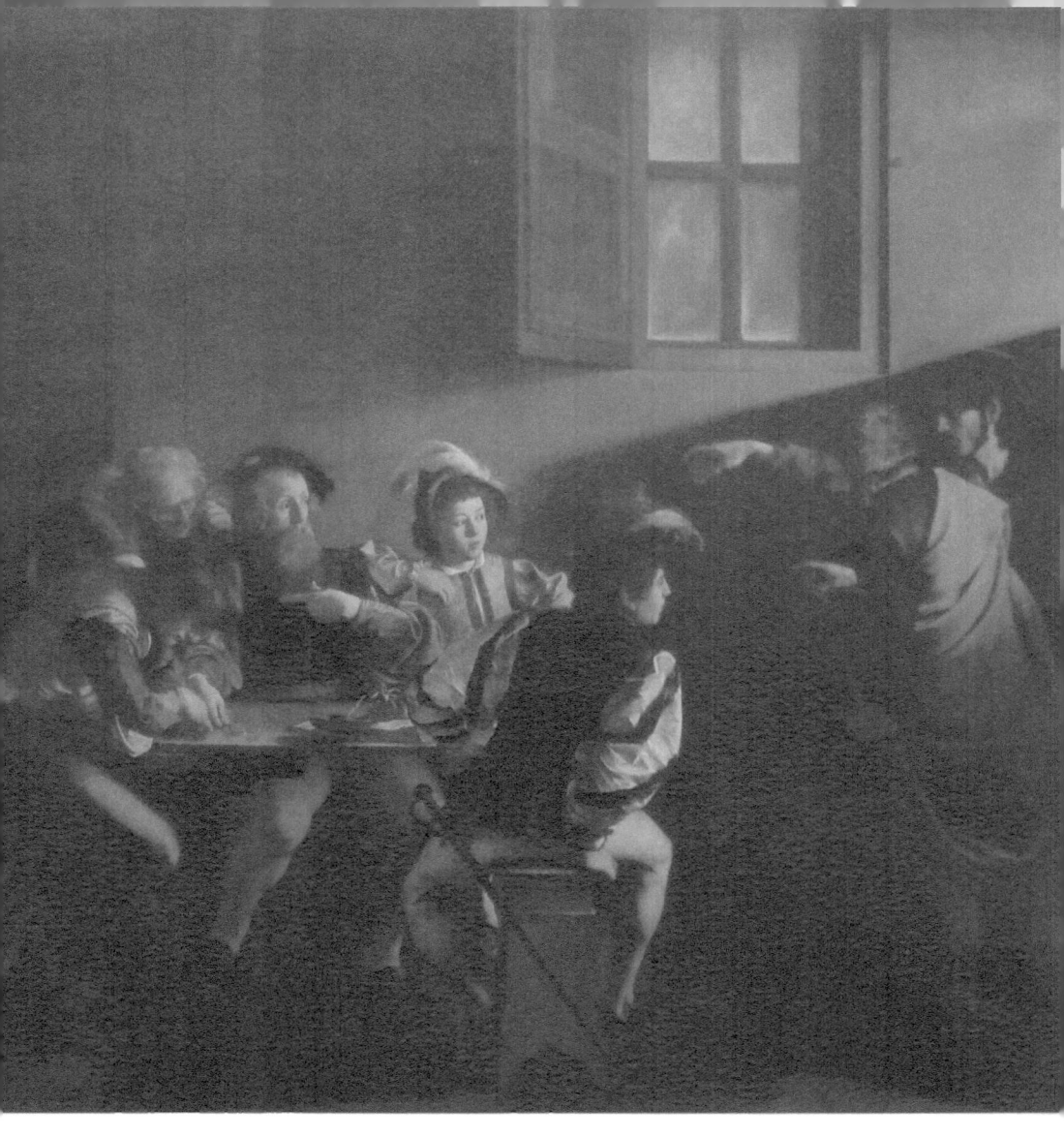

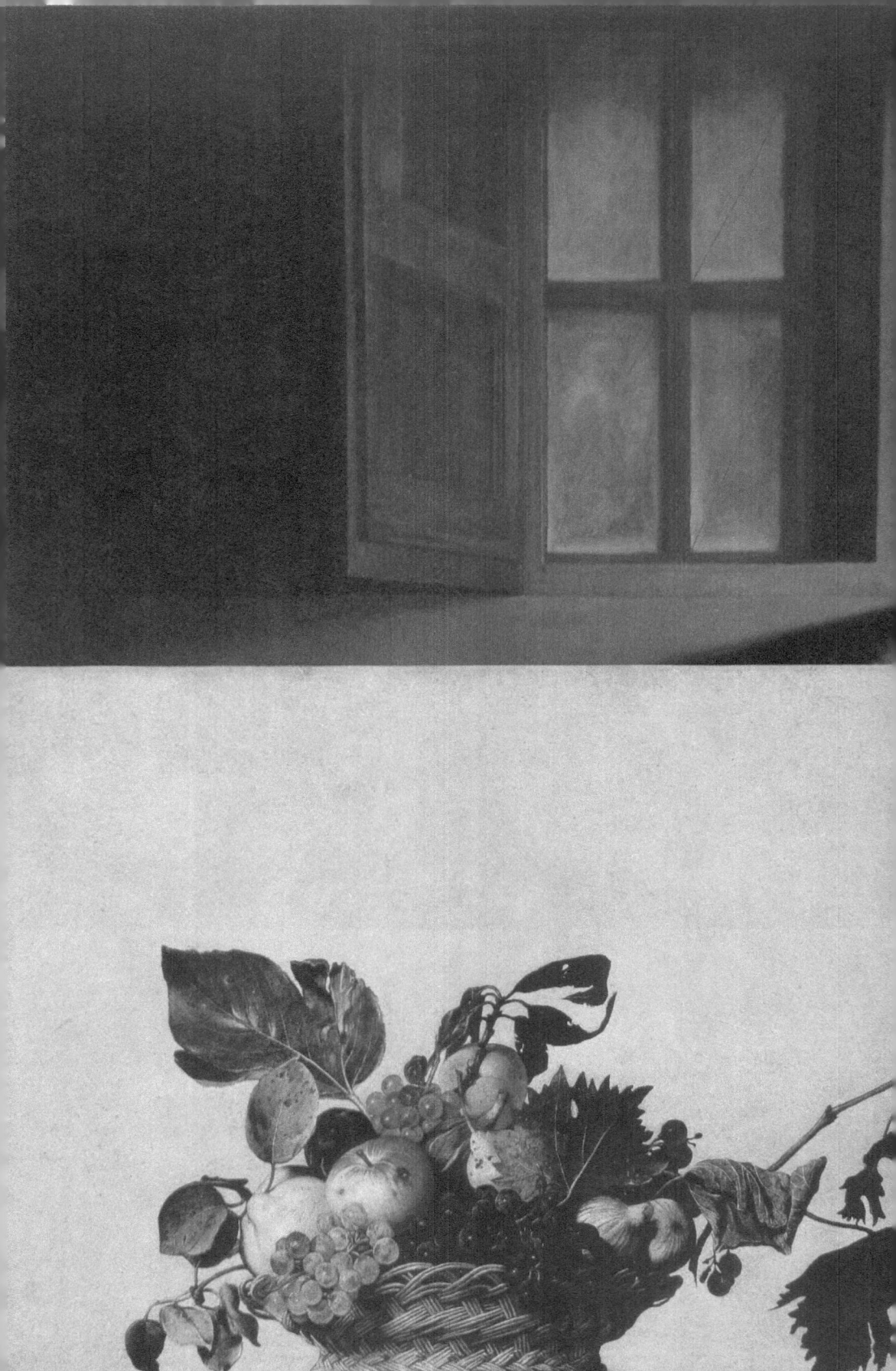

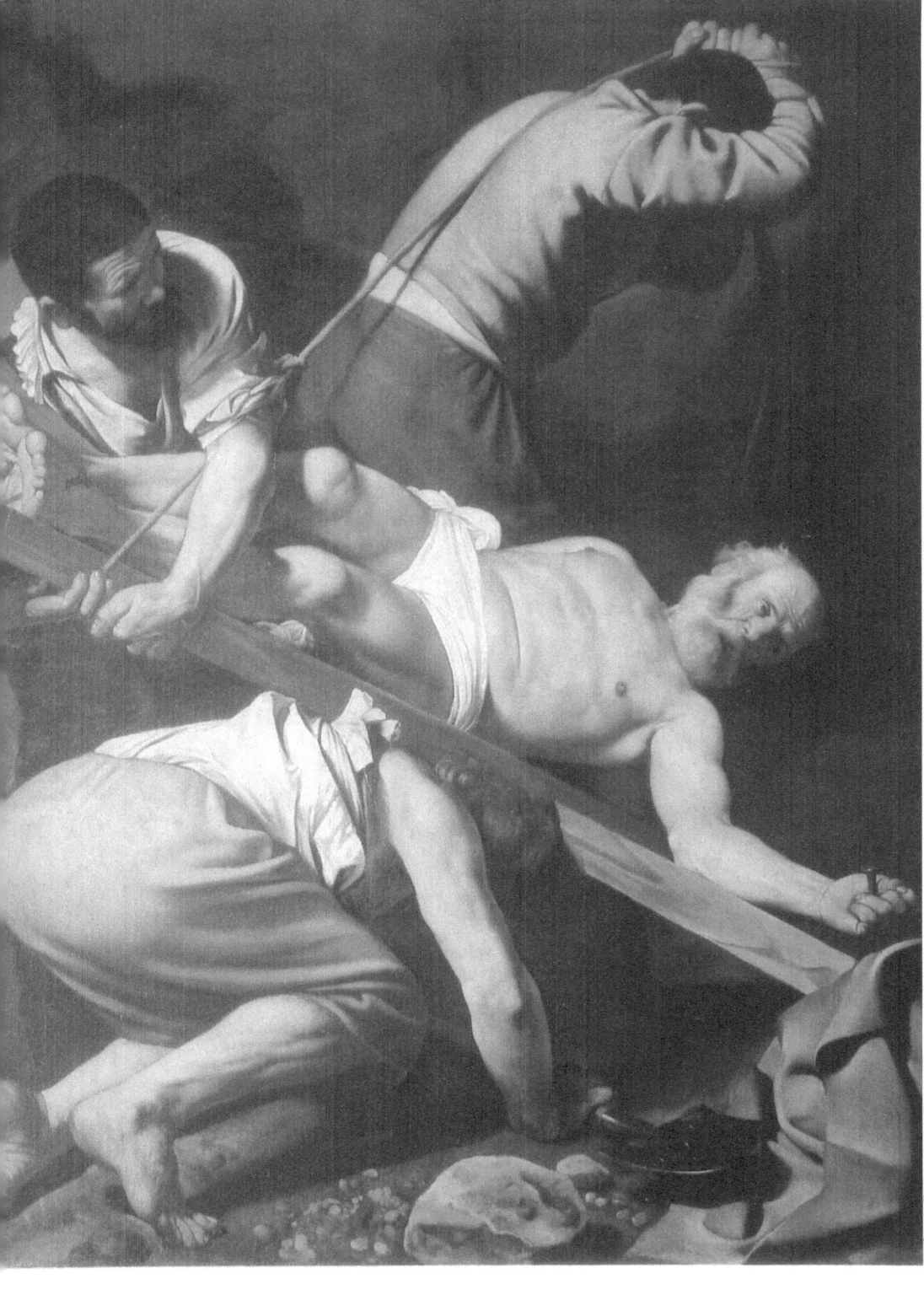

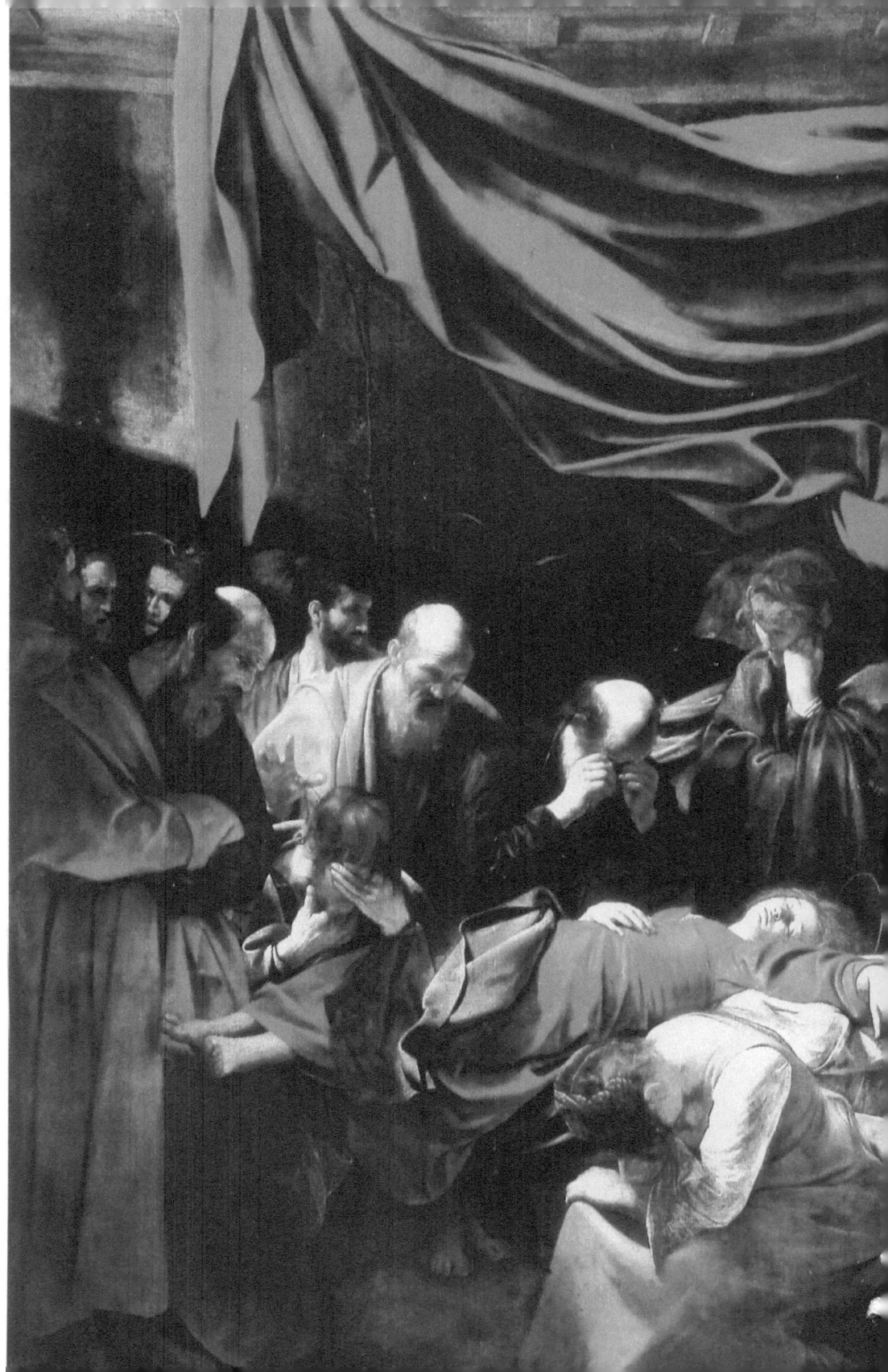

presented in these terms. He additionally accomplishes this without metaphor or rhetoric, but directly through strength of his very own composition of space.

The Virgin, having just died, extends her arm outside the picture plane. It becomes an arrow that hits the viewer as much as the laments of a woman beside us. Often in Caravaggio the proscenium it is pierced with these diagonal and unbalanced vectors. Here the entire body of the Virgin appears to lift out of the bed and throw itself diagonally across the picture plane. One can also refer to the diagonal cross of "Crucifixion of St. Peter" at S. Maria at Piazza del Popolo of 1602 and to the plinth that pushes forth like a prow toward the viewer in "The Entombment of Christ" in the Vatican Museums of 1602-1604. Further examples are the famous hand of Christ calling Matthew to the Contarelli Chapel of 1600; not to mention the table of the players literally in the balance and suspended in the space in the same picture of the "Calling of St. Matthew". The combinations of elements in precarious balance between inside and outside and the diagonal penetrations of the proscenium thereby destroy the classical roundness of the composition, tending to break apart the very idea of representation as separated performances. This diagonal destruction is "sword strike" (as it is physically depicted in "Judith Beheading Holofernes" at the National Gallery of Ancient Art of Rome of 1599 which in addition to the diagonal and the being barely in balance also manifests horror).

From Below

There is an interesting relationship between Caravaggio and the architecture of his time.

> I am unable to forget the image of Rome's atmosphere of bright noon sun, during the summery solstice; and Caravaggio, young, in his first or second summer on Rome's midday streets, amidst the deepening shadows extended on palaces and churches, and, against these shadows, the unexpected flashes of light, apparitions, of a swollen column, a slice of

cornice. (…) Caravaggio found this luminous world of architecture in the classical factories and those sixteenth century buildings that in those years were being built and from the very Lombard and Ticinese architects who worked in Rome. [And then the wealth of the detail as much in Caravaggio as in the architecture of the time…] Squeezing different areas in the tightest of times – varied paths, wandering, releasing from one apex to the other in a numerous polygon, (…) in a small space, a world is condensed. [6]

Building further upon the writings of architect Luigi Moretti, Giulio Carlo Argan in 1952 begins his volume on Francisco Borromini (Bissone, September 25, 1599 - Rome, August 3, 1667), with a series of analogies between the Ticinese architect and Caravaggio; despite the difference of a generation that separates them. (Caravaggio was born in Milan on September 29, 1571, according to the latest acquisitions of documents, and died in Porto Ercole, July 18 1610). The analogies study "his Lombardic origin, his arrival to Rome at a young age, his rebellion against the official artistic atmosphere, his bitter and conflictive nature, his restless existence and his despairing death".[7] However, both the unforgettable elements of atmosphere evoked by Moretti, and the differences that help us understand the facts from a historical-critical point of view, in my view, leave unsolved a strong relationship between Borromini and Caravaggio. Let us try to understand it via comparison.

Francesco Borromini generates his architectures in a new and heretical way (stated also by Bernini).[8] His method does not rely on the juxtaposition of parts but rather, creates a montage of architectural elements, (the wall, the beam structure, encompassing arches, the ring of the cupola, the clerestory, the dome), similar to renaissance architecture, but innately of movement of wrapping and centripetal forms that transforms the architectonic elements weaving them into the space. A continuous organism is created this way instead of a composition of overlapped and juxtaposed parts. The Chapel of Sant'Ivo is the work in which one sees more clearly this formative thought process of Borromini while, by contrast, Gian

Lorenzo Bernini explores the process of juxtaposition, (for example in the Church of S. Maria of the Assumption of Ariccia), and supplies a clear precedent (and prior to him, naturally, much renaissance architecture).

Let us return to Caravaggio. In order to better understand his revolutionary impact it would be enough to compare a painting of his with one of the analogous painter Annibale Carracci.[9] I will refer here to the painting dedicated to the Madonna of Loreto. Carracci employs a composition of juxtaposition in which the various iconographic components, (the famous house of the "Madonna of Loreto", her assumption composed centrally on the canvas, the angels encircling her), are depicted one detached from the other in a composition of symmetrical assembly in the mystical space of the heavens. Traditional iconography in Caravaggio is turned upside down by the depiction of an everyday scene. A woman with a child receives two pilgrim beggars from the house of the "Madonna di Loreto". This house is abbreviated simply to a door threshold. The everyday space is characteristically asymmetrical; providing a dynamic composition combined with chiaroscuro lighting, in contrast to the central composition and homogenous light of Carracci.

Let us explore here a structural aspect of the thought process of painting and to return to the relationship Borromini- Caravaggio. The key of Borromini's method, its basis being heretical, is in its technique of employing a cumulative visual build-up from below towards the above and not from the above towards the low. The architectonic elements move in a continuous motion from the low towards high, not a cupola dome that covers, protects and descends from the heavens but an earthly composition, beginning with geometric motifs of the plan that rotate and transform themselves arriving to spiral of the clerestory to then launch the dome's sphere towards the sky.

Returning to Caravaggio's painting, one notes that the principle composition is analogous and for this reason new and thus heretical! Caravaggio begins the composition at the feet of the beggar. The dirty and calloused feet are important not only from the point of

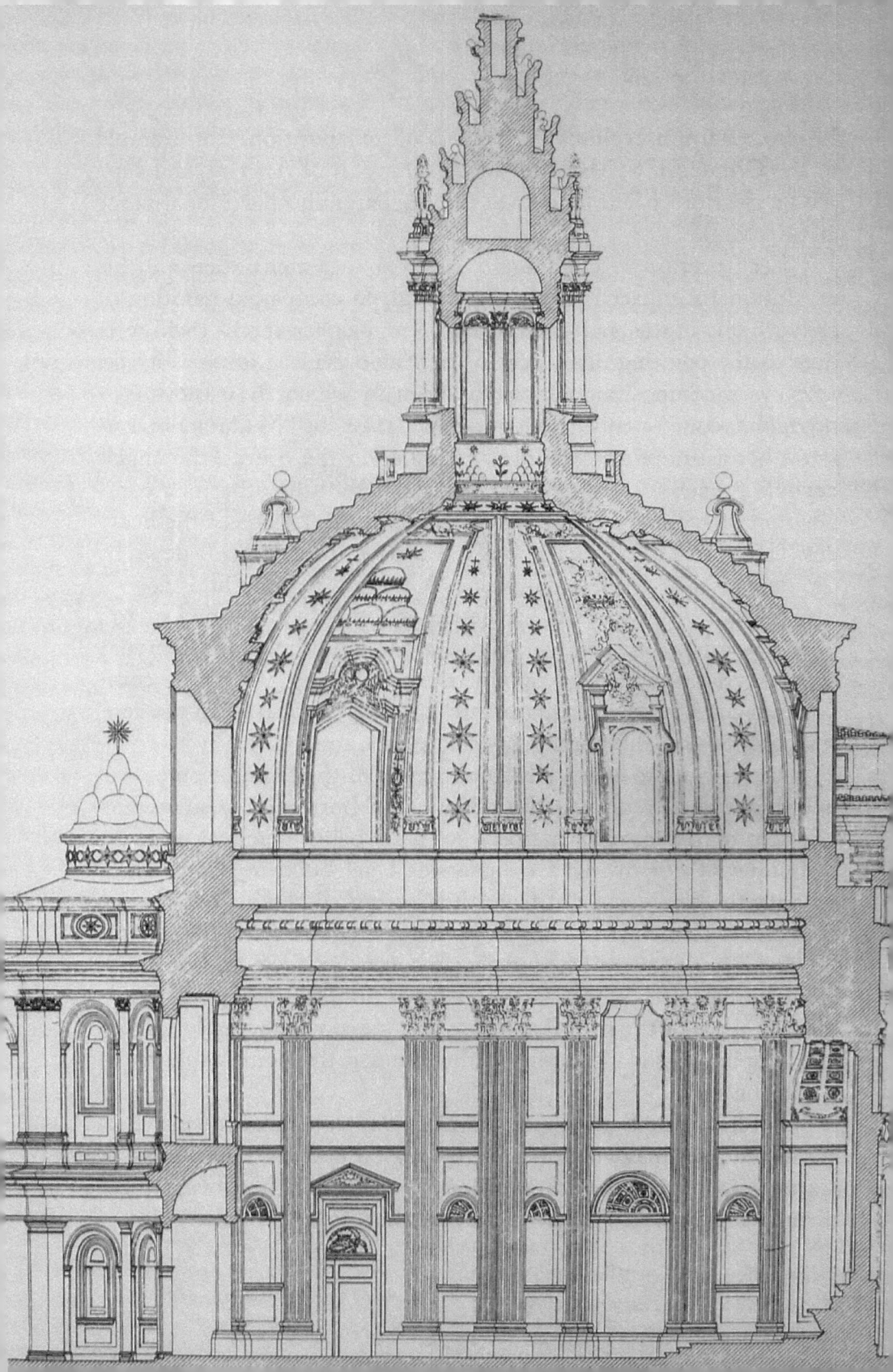

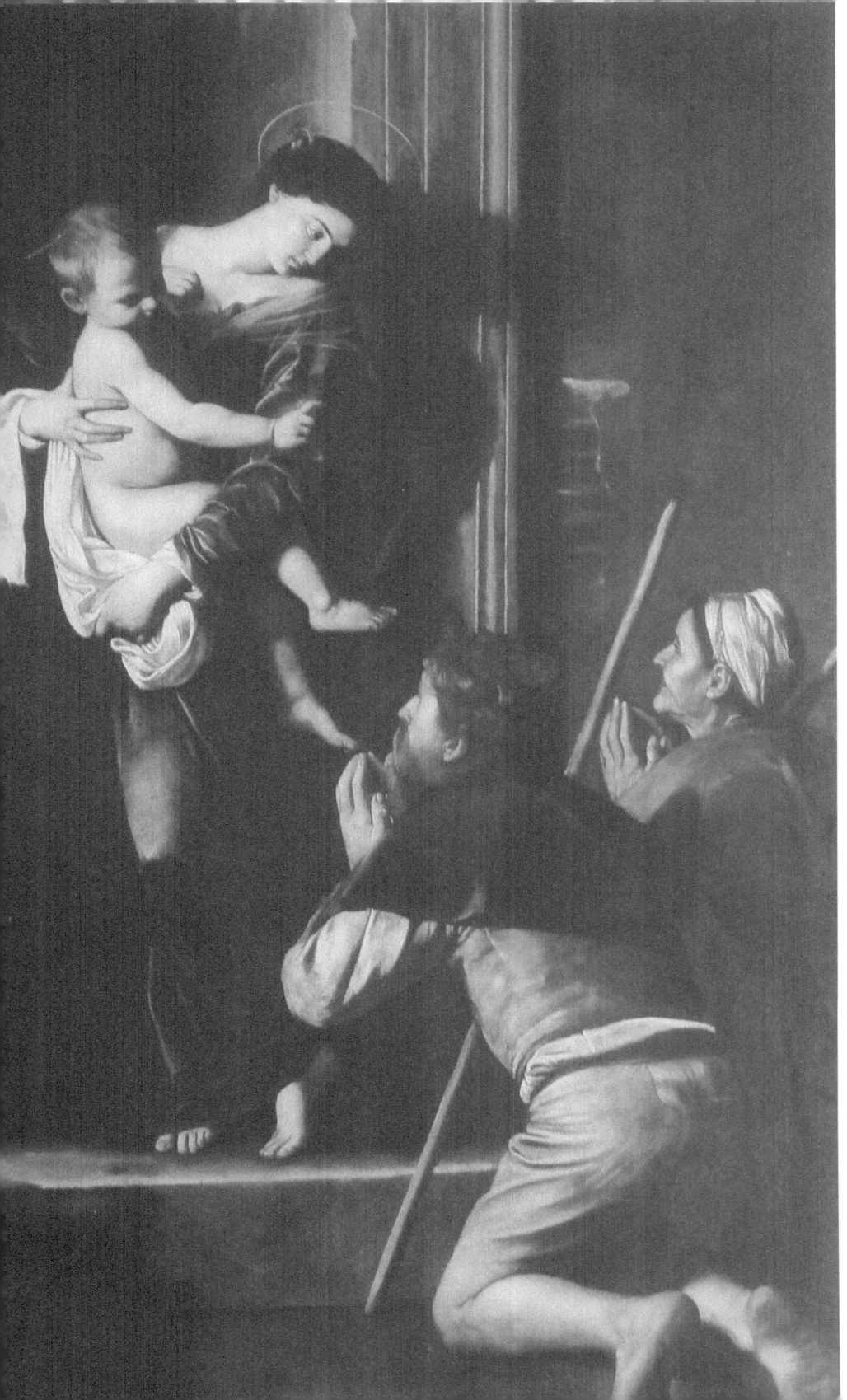

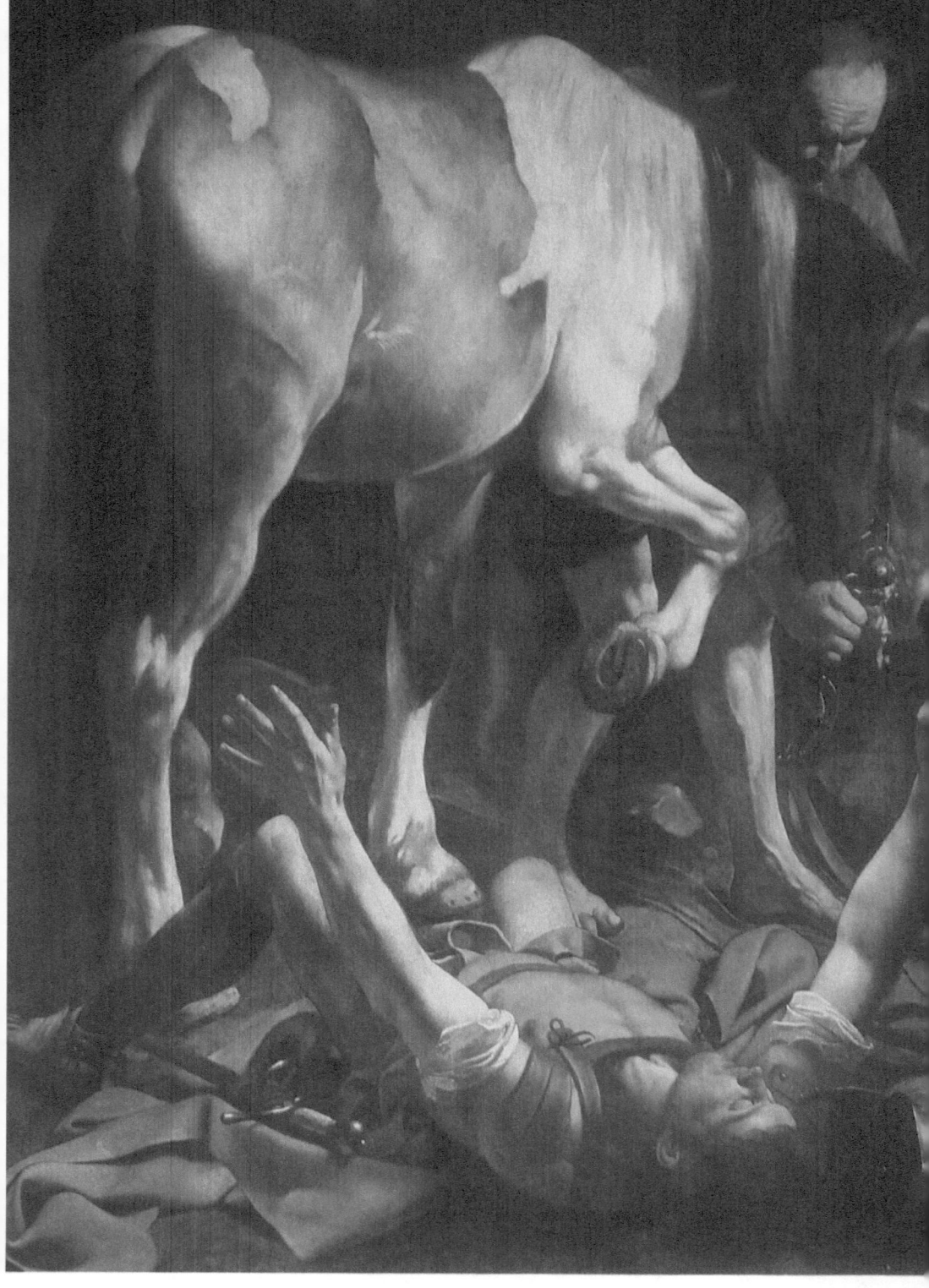

view of content and expression, but also from a deep structural point of structuring giving movement to the picture. Those same feet placed low in the composition, from the composition from below toward an upward movement bringing one to the face of Lena. This is in complete contrast to Annibale Carracci, opposite to the approaches of Bernini, but in line with the same principles, the same innovative structure and same movement of Borromini.

Was it not Galileo who taught that man now watches the firmament from below? We will return to this.

In Caravaggio, and this goes without saying, operating from below is found again in other powerful masterpieces. One can refer to both works in the Church of Santa Maria del Popolo: "The Conversion of Saint Paul" thrown to earth in the lowland of the picture with the open arms and again in the "Crucifixion of Saint Peter". You will notice the same principle exactly: composed from below!

Flash

Whoever has viewed a Michelangelo Merisi has noticed foremost the use of light. Or better said, the use of shadow vs. the use of light. Caravaggio literally destroys the use of light and recreates light. And if there is a sense to this word and its many metaphoric meanings (to view under a different light, to see the light etc) this "is" Michelangelo Merisi from Caravaggio.

Let us make a comparison. In an Antonello da Messina light is one of the new world of perspective, of the window frame, the figure of the Saint or the Madonna placed under a universal light source that emerges cloak-like from the sky; modeled in the faintest chiaroscuro forms and lost in a landscape of bluish clouds. Caravaggio extinguishes the lights in his room, pulls away the cloak, opens up proscenium and suspends his world into total darkness. His actors, moving as if they were two dimensional in the thickness of the canvas, are suddenly exposed without warning to a flash of light. The new light, the modern light of Michelangelo Merisi evolves into a flash that slices the scene.

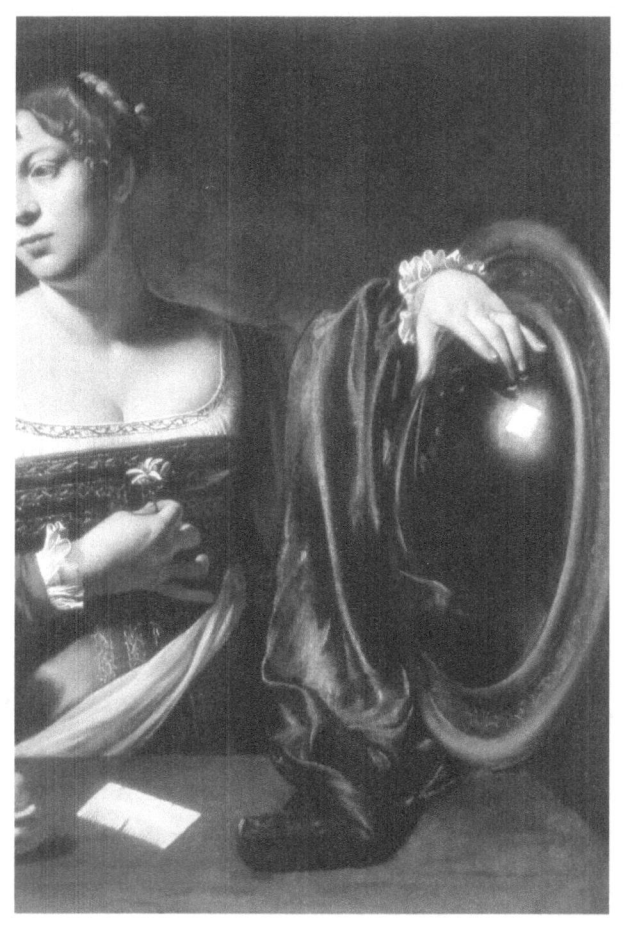

But why destroy light in order to create of a new one? It is because they have as much to do with the use and as well as the questioning of the new camera obscura reflective and projective qualities. It is an instrument that literally enables one to see the entire world under a different light. Let us now enter the very center of this text.

The Mirror

Abandon the old perspective frame, throw it out without mercy, destroy it. Take up instead a great flat mirror. Instead of painting upon the sketch that I would have made with the grid of my frame, I will paint the subject in real time, but not from life but as it is projected in the mirror!

I have a great advantage, in regards to reality, having the reflection flattened upon the mirror. I can create, as if I was a register, the poses, attitudes and the lighting of my subject and see it in the flattened representation of the mirror as if it was practically a ready picture, already realized. This staged and choreographed creation is a large part of my process and my final success depends heavily on it. Once the scene is decided I must naturally paint it upon the canvas.

I could certainly transfer it all using points, with the system of the grid, but it is very long and perhaps incorrect in concept. I want to eliminate this cursed system. I think to use the calipers that my architect friend Onorio Longhi possesses. With a calipers, beautifully large, I measure my subject and its parts, but sketch precisely upon the mirror! Then I invent a quick method that is based on the use of "two large calipers". With one set of calipers, my assistant measures on the mirror the distance from the point A to that B and, I with the other calipers, record the dimension and transfer it to the canvas. I can ,in this way, quickly transfer the image on the mirror to the canvas and paint in myself, or Mario disguised as Bacchus or the players or even Mario and the gypsy or Margherita as Magdalen and in this case I tilt the same mirror in order to see what the distortion does to the picture.

The "agonized, ectstatic and regal one"[10] Michelangelo Merisi, the young twenty-five year old, that gives violent swings to life, wants to arrive with culture, inspiration, talent, technique (and with the sword) to the pinnacle of society ; abandoning the poverty in which he lived until to being sheltered in a hostel for poor,[11] adopts this technique of the mirror. The invention, naturally, is only one of the factors that determine his aesthetic. It is not the mirror itself, as it is likewise not the perspective frame that determine anything. But it is precisely the looking into the mirror in real time that changes everything because it is very different to observe within a mirror than through a perspective grid. To observe in the mirror signifies to throw overboard the static immobility of the canvas, to refuse to think of a world "beyond the window" separated from us; not to intellectualize idealized scenes on paper, but to create them in reality. To exist within the mirror means to be taken directly, to redefine color that becomes the protagonist, to have a light of combined opalescence and reflection. The mirror implies that painting speaks about "representation of truth", not of reality itself, but in a self-reflexive vein. That is often associated to the emergence, precisely, of a new, "modern" condition. But this is not enough, another dramatic leap is about to happen.

Camera Obscura

One day one of the important intellectuals of the end of the Roman 1500's runs into one of my reflected pictures. My cardinal knows of it all. He is the ambassador of the Pope of the Medici Grand Duke, Palazzo Madama is his home and he is friends with many philosophers, musicians, scientists. He owns the book of Giovanni Batista Della Porta (1584 Magiae naturalis sive de miraculis rerum naturalium). Cardinal Del Monte receives me into his house, hosts me, pays me in exchange for my paintings. And he wants, like the Duke of Urbino more than a century before, to create an atelier of knowledge and science. Together we discuss, not only on the mirror and its use, but on a strange phenomenon. And that is; on the "camera obscura", which is to say that if I place a flower in a dark room, from that very flower a ray of light passes that "projects" the outside on a part of the room as if there, on the wall of the dark room, there was a mirror, even if the mirror is not there. But all it appears only for a moment. For a moment it is visible

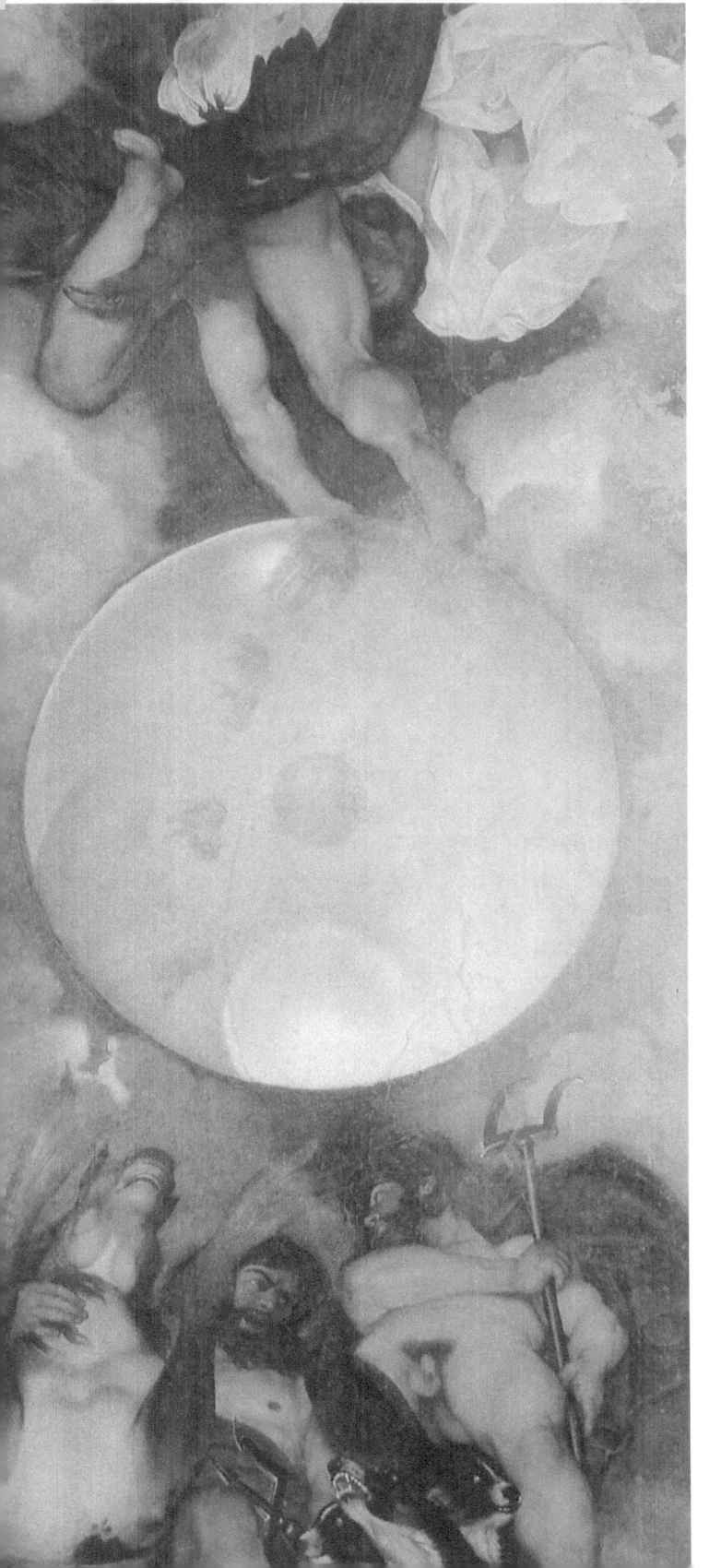

and lit and then it disappears, the camera is an instrument that captures this moment.... The same strong contrast between light and shadow through which the mechanism works makes me look differently at myself, my friends, my time, as if time itself were truly dramatically changed!

The camera fascinates me even technically because I quickly imagine that if put the canvas in that point in which the image is reflected perhaps I could trace directly and perhaps paint by tracing and no longer use the system of the calipers! Del Monte also introduces me to his Florentine friend Galileo who besides having made the prodigious invention of the telescope, of which my cardinal he possesses one of the few, is a true expert of the lens. The lens bases itself on the properties of the curve and this concavity and convexity, instead only reflecting like a normal mirror, makes "rays converge" and of course magnifies or reduces exactly as it happens in the telescope. Now I discover an extraordinary thing: if I use a curved mirror and not a flat one as I did before, the image not only comes obviously enlarged or reduced, but it comes to being p r o j e c t e d onto the wall: and is recreated on the wall precisely because the rays converge instead of dispersing themselves to the infinite as it happens in a flat mirror! If I place a canvas at this point , I could truly paint there, tracing the projection!

Little by little I discover how to make that "camera obscura" of painting that one of my biographers with an eye for science (he was also a doctor) practically already described. The subject must be strongly lit and with high contrast. I reflect the subject on a flat mirror (it can always be useful to me to also employ the technique of the calipers), but above all I reflect the image on the flat mirror onto a smaller curved mirror. I make this reflection on the curved mirror converge onto a lens that allows a precise focusing and I project it onto my canvas within the camera obscura! Here I can paint, marking the contours of the subject in order to make reference points that allow me to re-enact the exactly same pose after a pause. I can paint quick first drafts in white lead, in order then to pass to the color.

My times are dangerous ones. I must keep secret this camera obscura of mine because jealous colleagues sooner or later will take advantage of it, but above all because they might accuse me of witchcraft and I run the risk of ending up at Campo de Fiori like Giordano Bruno.

Through this invention, a mature Caravaggio is born that will revolutionize sight. All that we have made note of returns. Before all is the necessity of a strong light source as well as deep shadow, and then the captured moment, the precarious balance, the break from the frame. Caravaggio substitutes from the fixed canvas and uniform light, the momentary blinding of the flash, he creates a stage and has his figures project themselves into and beyond it. His whole life is in precarious balance, his paintings, his sense of space also because "materially" the entire system of the camera obscura balances itself on a single point, a single moment, and with very little this equilibrium can be shattered and sink into nothing. But the moments that Caravaggio creates are the first in the new world: men speak of themselves, of their being real, of their human wretchedness, but to aspire nonetheless to their small existence, reflected in a figure projected in a camera obscura.

Ask the Dust

Those familiar with Caravaggio's paintings, recognize in them actors that may every so often appear on the television. These actors are his protagonists and each time they play a different role. Mario (Minniti) at first a lute player, then a tavern card player in "The Calling of Saint Matthew", then a youth fleeing from a murder scene; Anna (Bianchini) as Magdalen or Madonna in flight in Egypt; Lionello (Spada) as card player and then murderer of Saint Matthew; Lena (Maddalena Antognetti) as Mary at the threshold or aiding the child to kill a serpent; Cecco (Francesco Boneri) from whom follows a full development of child to young man (angel with Matthew, David, Isac, John the Baptist etc.) and many others: "Francesco" (who besides his namesake saint, is Saint Paul or Christ), "Matteo" (who from time to time represents the saint, or Saint Jerome or Abraham or Saint Paul) or Narciso (of the same named painting in the Galleria d'Arte Antica, but also as angel in the flight from Egypt and card player in the taverns), or Fillide (Melandroni) as

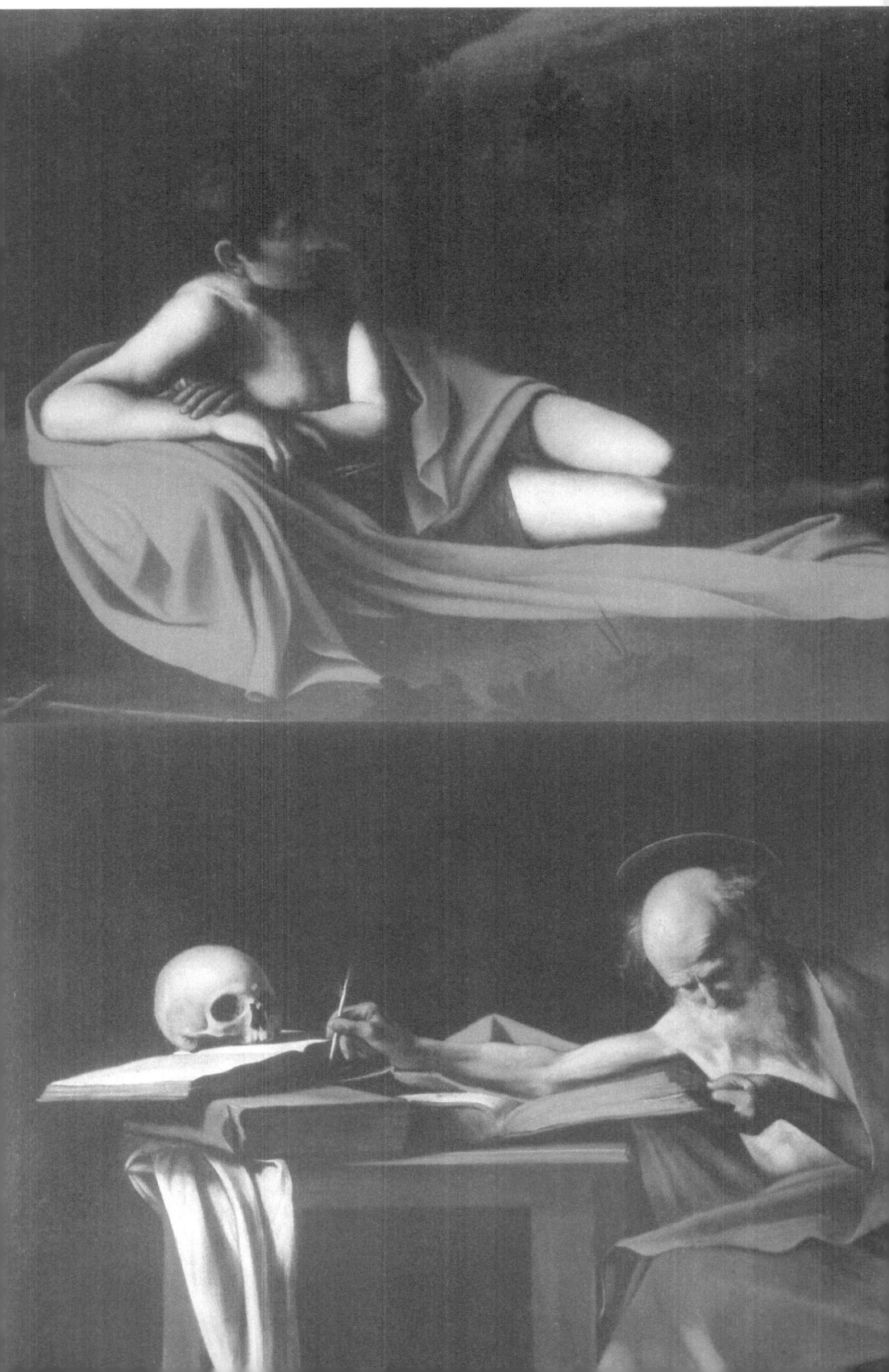

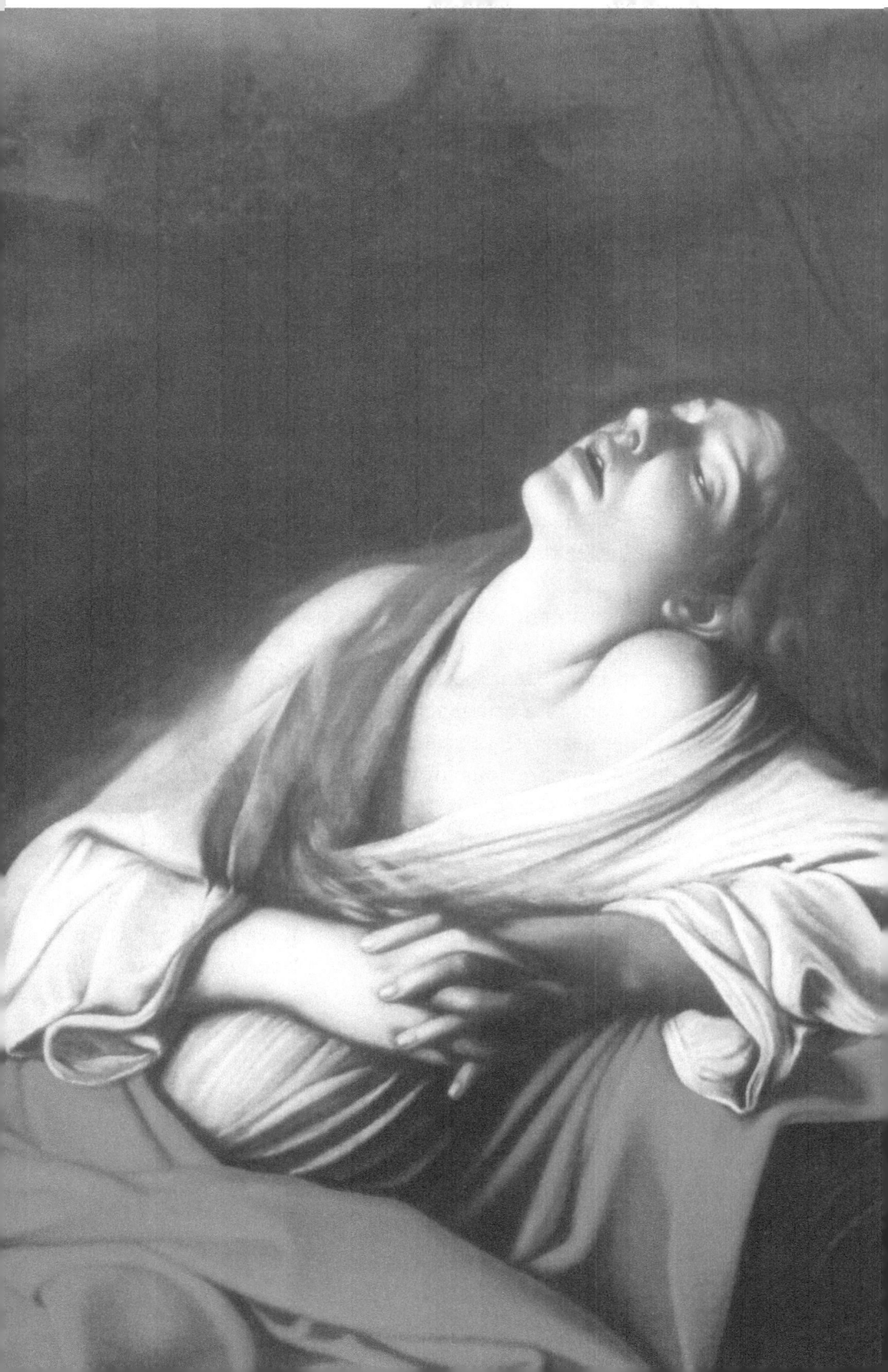

Saint Catherine or as Judith. However, if there exists a spatiality of precarious balance between inside and outside, if this space is called a proscenium mixing both at and the mundane, if the characters themselves are real people, then the painter is also a director and the camera obscura is his principle instrument.

And here is the novelty – a new twist – between instrument and revolutionary vision. Caravaggio is a realist director, a kind of hyper-realist to the level of pulp. Its actors do not have to "primarily" enact the scenes that are commissioned, more than the architecture of an architect serve to provide a roof and a space to inhabit. Or course, the paintings serve to tell the commissioned narrative, but they are very out there, incomparably elsewhere. Michelangelo Merisi uses saints and martyrs, answers to the required iconografic demands but it is something other that he speaks to us. His actors speak of a real life, truthful life. True in the violent defense of a different I (as different were Leonardo and Michelangelo), true in dust covered feet, or in the seductive smiles of the musicians or in fruit both beautiful and worm-eaten or in Lena's incredibly suggestive pose or the dramatically violent one of a brutal act.

The single appearance in scene of these street actors would be enough to destroy the previous idea of the painting because with the actors and beyond the actors is the director himself who becomes primary, by now unrefuted, protagonist of the painting. Painting now becomes always a complicit self-portrait: ideas, tensions, acquaintances, characters, friends and lovers are all together protagonists not of a composed scene, but of a personal reality of a truthful I
. It lives and sees in new way, with a new instrument. The view of heavens, divine light, dogmas descended from above towards defenseless and silent men, is inverted by Galileo's. A small man is now rooted to the ground and aims his eye on high with a telescope. The view is from below: built on facts, science and the knowledge of complex systems. From below towards on high. Caravaggio reveals to the world, for the first time, this new view from below using Galileo's very same lens.

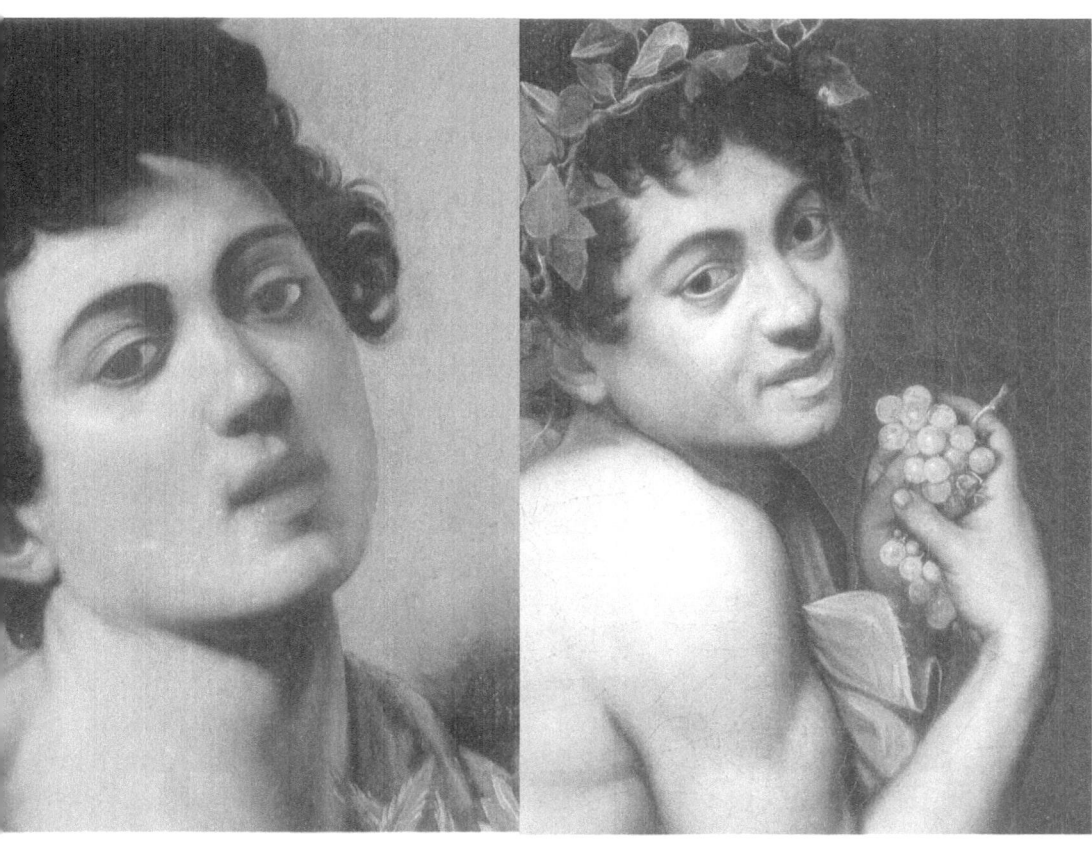

Caravaggio's use of the mirror has been verified. The little things left among the inventory of abandoned objects in his Roman studio, despite the damage of an inexplicably demolished roof, are "a large mirror (...) and a mirrored shield".[12] This curved mirror is painted by Caravaggio in the painting "Martha and Mary Magdalene" (1597, Detroit Institute of Arts).[13]

Caravaggio, in another confirmed fact, was detained one night near Piazza Navona by the police bearing two sets of calipers. These were probably large in size given that they alarmed the guardsmen. "He carried a sword without license and a pair of calipers".[14] This last quote is the first text ,(to the best of my knowledge)[15], that associates the use of calipers and the use of a mirror with painting and proposed the theory on why he required "two" sets of calipers.

Another certainty is that Caravaggio's patron, the cardinal Francesco Maria Borbone Del Monte, researched projections and lenses and mirrors. He personally knew Galileo and was familiar with all the details of his lenses and with one of the few telescopes that was constructed. The early scientist Giacomo della Porta had written a treaty, of which we mentioned,[16] in which he outlined the concepts of the camera obscura. It is fairly certain that the scholarly Del Monte was familiar with the text and would have spoken of it to his painter. It is highly improbable to me that Del Monte and Caravaggio would not have wanted to experiment and build a camera obscura, as it is likewise to David Hockney.[17]

His very own contemporaries practically describe his camera obscura. The following was written by Giacomo Mancini a few years after the death of the painter.

> From this very school comes the concept of single source lighting from above without glare as it would be in a room of black walls lit from a single window, and thus, having the highlights with shadows very clear and dark, it would bring depth to the painting, but in an unnatural way, neither made in the manner of, nor in the thought of past centuries or

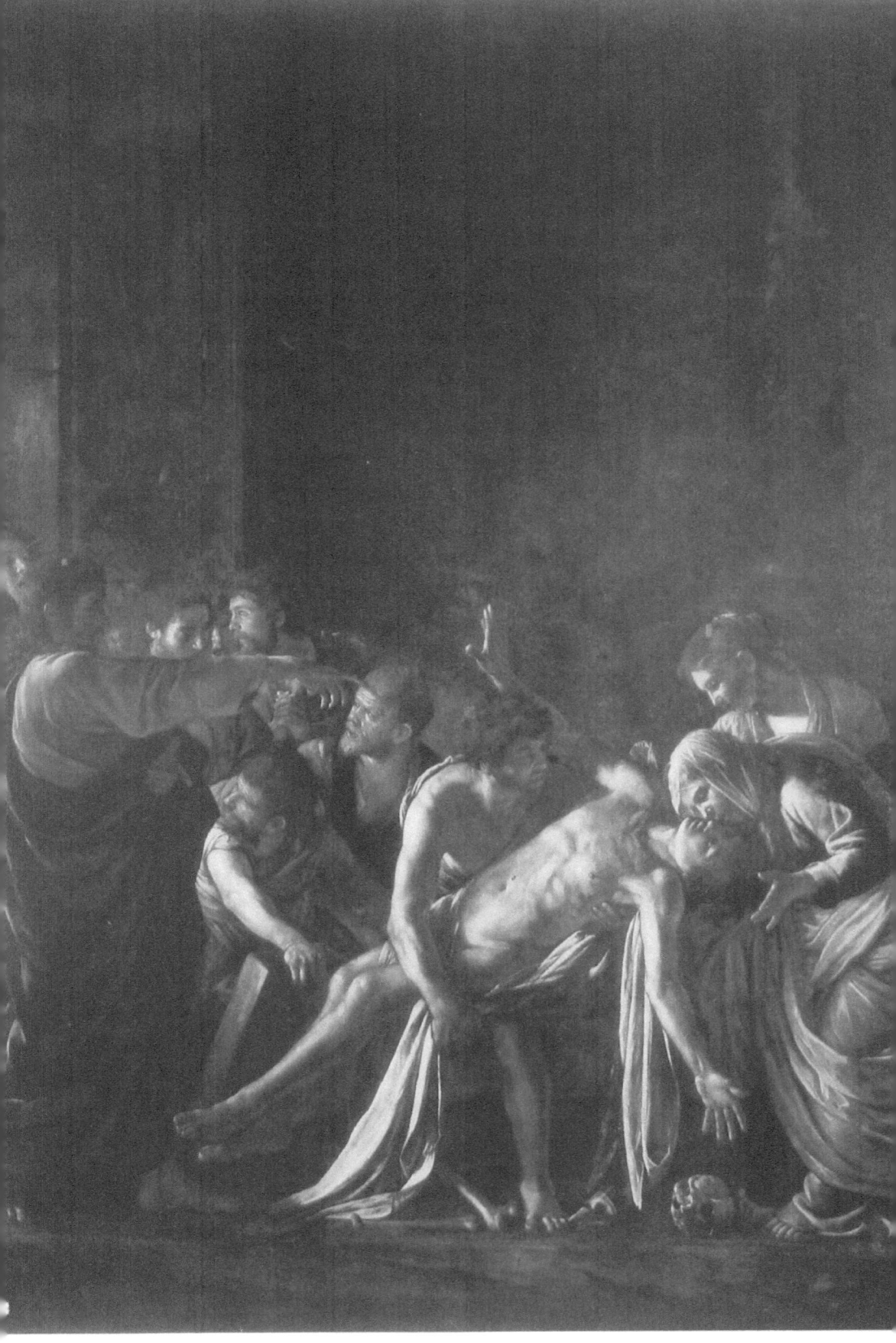

painters, like Rafael, Titian, Correggio and others. This
school examines in this manner from life which it always
references directly while working.... 18

Another aspect of Caravaggio is that he did not "draw". He in-
scribed the canvas with strong border lines, markers or control lines,
and then proceeded rapidly with a type of pre-painting made with
white lead on a dark ground. This is a well recognized technique
confirmed by several scholars; in particular by Mina Gregori.[19] It can
be discerned in x-rays although some of these markers are visible to
the naked eye. It is very probable that these markers served as control points to verify the exact position of the model during the sit-
ting or to re-position them after a break. On the other hand, some
of the strange and inexplicable distortions in the work are possibly
the result of an erroneous re-positioning of the model in regards of
the markers. The collection of these multiple facts bring one to confirm Caravaggio's use of the mirror and above all his use of the camera obscura. It is practically impossible, given the facts, that he had
not experimented with it.

I would like to add to these observations some additional de-
ductive elements that I believe new, and should the reader remain
with doubts, further support Caravaggio's use of both mirror and
camera obscura.

No painting of Caravaggio is known prior to his age of 23 years.
This is considered already an advanced age for a painter of his time.
One of the first works, "Boy Peeling a Pear" of 1592, appears reflected in a mirror as it is almost certainly in the famous "Bacchino
Malato" ; now unanimously considered a self-portrait and to be
mirrored.[20] There also exists the portrait of Mario as "Bacchus" hold-
ing a goblet with his left hand. Why are there no known pictures of
Caravaggio prior to this date? A possible theory is that previous
works may have been rendered unrecognizable due to the radical
change in his style through the use of the mirror (rendered even
more precise with the use of calipers) .

How come Caravaggio does not paint with the al-fresco medium which was common technique of the painters of his time? The answers seems obvious to this logic of thinking. The only painting that is found on a wall is actually a canvas commissioned for the Casino dell'Aurora in Rome in the alchemy lab of Cardinal Del Monte.

The daring rise from below towards on high of "Jupiter, Neptune and Pluto", seems to represent three full figure self-portraits realized with a mirror placed on the floor.

Some of the few portraits painted by Caravaggio (i.e. the portrait of monsignor Maffeo Barberini) appears very little Caravaggio-like in their features. The hypothesis being that Caravaggio could not use the full spectrum of his technique when he had to paint an important personage. On the other hand, the fact that he relied on narrow group of friends for models (and at times used same model to depict multiple characters in the same painting) would also explain the use of a camera obscura. The obvious reason would be not to expose, unless absolutely necessary, his technique under many points of view that could perceive it as threatening.

In the late phase of its painting, when he often painted hidden and protected in convents and monasteries, his style changes and becomes looser either for expressive reasons or for the lack of a camera obscura.

Narcissus in time

In conclusion, let us return to the passage by Roberto Longhi with which we started.

> Thus he came his own empirical experience with the "camera obscura, and this was nearly a scientific discovery – in any case his personal experience". What is most surprising is that this occurred at the times of Della Porta and, eventually, of Galileo. His obstinate deference to realism could be confirmed in the ingenuous belief that was `the eye of the camera' watching him and suggesting it all to him. He must have

been bewitched many times in front of that `natural magic ', and what must have most surprised him was that the human figure was not necessary to the mirror, if exited from its field, it continued to reflect the tilted floor, the shadow on the wall, the fallen ribbon on the ground. It is not difficult to understand that he could achieve to this level of realism by proceeding directly toward mirroring reality. He achieved the blank slate of the time's culture of painting, preparing the sketches in pencil and paper and via historical-mythological reference and stylized abstraction; it had elaborated a division in classes of the representation that, transposed socially, could not dream toward higher steps.'.[21]

The powerful key to Longhi's passage is the idea that the mirror continues to reflect despite our absence! The perspective frame does not see without the human eye: It partitions and frames but it does not create the image; the mirror instead does! The mirror reflects notwithstanding. For the mirror "the human figure was not necessary ..., if exited this from its field, it continued to reflect the tilted floor, the shadow on the wall, the fallen ribbon on the ground...." This schism brings an object's autonomy to the very center of representation. This is a birth of objective, analytic, reflexive vision that is other than itself and other than man himself, becoming what will be asserted and later called modernism future centuries.[22]

Narcissus (the subject of a painting by Caravaggio at the Barberini Gallery in Rome) looks upon himself; melancholy and meditative in a black mirror of water: he appears about to fall and his image formed fleetingly.

Towards the end of the 1500's, Caravaggio feels that the time has run out. The time has ended of divine light as direction toward serenity, space and absolute time. Michelangelo is aware that modern time, perhaps beginning with him, is one of the moment, or the instant, of drama and of the crossroad. Every moment can be introduced as one of choice, of death or of life. Only the moment of a flash is our dim light of life, desire, possibility: only the moment in precarious balance choice "is".[23]

ENDNOTES

[1] Roberto Longhi, *Caravaggio*, Editori Riuniti, Rome 1952 pp. 64. Longhi whispers in this work that among the reasons for the revolutionary vision of Caravaggio there had been the use of a device. A device that is not only a mirror, to which the critic often refers in his writings, but of a true optical room; of a projection system strengthened with the use of one or more lenses. This follows an intuition that in the past few years has come to light through new studies of remarkable interest. I refer in detail to the volume by David Hockney, *Secret Knowledge Rediscovering the Lost Techniques of the Old Masters*, Thames& Hudson, London 2006 (first edition 2001, Italian edition Electa 2002). This volume has provoked wide interest and animated contrasting points of view. Hockney develops a simple and direct thesis, that it is equivalent to saying "the King is nude". Scandalizing many art historians that very rarely interest themselves in viewing devices, the author, in extreme synthesis, posits that from approximately 1425 and until a good part of the 1800's some artists have used projection devices generating a kind of "optical" technique of the painting. Hockney explains it thus. Taking a curved mirror (that has a focal convergence of rays, instead of reflecting them in parallels) will magnify its subject. If this mirror reflects a well-lit image, the image will be able to be projected onto a wall. It will certainly be out of focus, but the image will effectively be projected! Hockney continues on to explain at this point, that if the technique is further developed (well illuminated subject, only a simple flower in a dark room, the use of a lens to focus and a 45 degrees mirror for the reflection of the image) , one has the an optical room - camera obscura. Hockney supports on this basis, that there is an entire development of painting that (but the text is very detailed) used this technique as an aid in order to create drawings and paint-

ings. To the obvious question: "But why was this technique thus held secret?" the author counters with the most serious danger of persecution and with the subsequent loosened grip of the Inquisition, one begins to effectively see in artist self portraits representations of the camera obscura among the artists devices. In this text, I will underline, as it will immediately become clear to the reader, the key concept: Caravaggio's device is not an ancillary technique, "magic trick" or "a prodigious invention" (that would allow in a semi-automatic mode for the seeds of his hyper-realistic painting), but on the contrary, it is an element of crisis, of difficulty and challenge that is imposed by birth of a new vision.

These themes have been issued prior to the printing of this volume (first edition lulu.com and Kappa 2007), in two of my writings: "Il Motivo di Caravaggio" published in Arch'it on October 15, 2007 and "Lo Strumento de Caravaggio" also in Arch'it on April 27, 2007. They are both available at http://architettura.supereva.com/coffebreak/.

[2] I owe this quote by the famous Paul Valery, *Eupalino o l'architetto*, Marseille1985 (first edition 1921) to my friend Antonello Marotta in his *Daniel Libeskind*, Edilstampa, Rome 2007. On the relationship between device, new vision and architecture, I recently published *The IT Revolution In Architecture, Thoughts on a Paradigm Shift* (in Italian published by Carocci editore in 2007 and in English by Lulu.com) of which I refer to previous reflections on the topic.

[3] Crisis, device and the very concept of "modernity" cannot but be intimately connected according to often discussed definition in *The IT Revolution In Architecture, Thoughts on a Paradigm Shift* (cit.) pp. 24-26. Caravaggio's device is the camera obscura. It is certainly not of an aseptic tool, but it is precisely this and the challenge for a new vision, one with a critical aesthetic eye.

It is a vision in which the device becomes the "incarnation of spirit, the materialization of thought: (as written by Alexandre Koyré, *Dal mondo del pressapoco all'universo della precisione*, Einaudi, Turin 2003 French edition 1961, p. 101, I credit the note of this text to my Maurizio Gargano).

[4] To provide a quick synopsis to younger readers, painting devices can be divided into two large categories: one belongs to the realm of the physical and material (techniques of execution, the type of structure and it's assembly, qualities of color, the consistencies of the medium etc.), but just as important as these material devices are the cognitive ones (philosophy,

rhetoric, symbolism, iconography and sciences). The laws of representation form part of this last category. The methods of perceiving and representing space is, from a specific point of view, the very heart of painting's evolution. The foremost example is the birth of the perspective grid at the start of the 1400's. The invention of perspective (and that being the method of representing two-dimensionally a depth of the space, through objective laws, reproducible and therefore scientific) initiated an enormous change in all of the arts. Caravaggio replaces this cognitive device, and its mode of representation, with a new vision. The change is total, all-encompassing, difficult and dramatic. It is a veritable "destruction" of what painting had been until to that moment (as said by the classical painter Nicolas Poussin: "Caravaggio was born in order to destroy painting" cited by Peter Robb, M the Enigma of Caravaggio , Oscar Mondadori, Milan 2001 first Australian edition Duffy & Snellgrove 1998 p. 18: "Monsieur Poussin [...] ne povoit rien souffrir du Caravage et disoit qu'il estait venu au monde pour destruire la Peinture").

Differing phases can be identified in the relationship between painting and the device of representation. The first is the revolutionary phase when one identifies the potential of the new representational device and through an arduous process a new logic and expression is found; the second phase is of affirmation and the subsequent fullness of meaning of its new mode of representation; the third is the birth of a critical eye upon the device and of its own limits, *but without yet knowing the next device that will lead to a new path* through this critical investigation. One can trace from this vantage point an arc of approximately 170 years than runs from the Trinity of Masaccio (1426) and the Revelation of Matthew by Caravaggio. Between the second and fourth decade of the 1400s in Florence, the new perspective vision is realized (Masaccio, Brunelleschi, Paolo Uccello), followed by a matured application (Piero della Francesca, Perugino, Antonello), however by the start of the 1500s research surpasses the paradigm of representation created through perspective, to place it in crisis with differing directions (Leonardo's atmosphere, Michelangelo's modeling, Giorgione's manipulation of tone, Pontormo's interlocking, Guilio Romano's hybridization, El Greco's distortions etc.).Caravaggio, however, does not belong to this phase labeled as "mannerism" by the art historian Arnold Hauser (*Il Manierismo*, Einaudi, Turin 1965), rather to the re-establishment of a substantially anti-perspective attitude and the start therefore of a cycle, no longer based on the cognitive device and of perspective representation, but exactly on the threshold of a new vision of reality that arrives from an investigation of the new "optical" parameters "opticians" and of projection.

[5] I refer to a "real" still life, in this case that of the Virgin, comparing her to the still life of a basket of fruit as "false" because it was very rare to have previously seen such a violent still life.

[6] Luigi Moretti, "Discontinuità dello spazio in Caravaggio", *Spazio*, n.5, 1951 credit goes to the architect Paola Ruotolo.

[7] Giulio Carlo Argan, *Borromini*, Mondadori, Milan 1952.

[8] "It is best to be a bad catholic, than a good heretic" attributed to Gian Lorenzo Bernini di Borromini (cited by Argan 1952 p. 18). On Borromini and Sant'Ivo I quote my essay "Il Motivo di Sant'Ivo", *Arch'it*, March 2 2005, http://architettura.supereva.com/coffeebreak/20050302/. And the most complete version in English "Interpretations of Borromini's Masterpiece at the Sapienza. The Reasons for Doubles and Other Considerations" Disegnare Idee e Immagini n. 39 December 2009. Bruno Zevi discusses in depth di Sant'Ivo reviews the notion of heresy in Borrominian architecture (in relation to the progression from below to on high in architecture). There is also a beautiful film by RAI on Borromini from 1972. I transcribed a part of it in "Linee Virtuali. Da Cannareggio a Castelvecchio", Arch' it, December 11, 2004, http://architettura.supereva.com/coffeebreak/20041211/.

[9] Caravaggio's painting dated 1604-1605 is in Sant'Agostino, the one by Carracci dated 1603-1604 is at Sant'Onofrio, also in Rome. Robb 2001 p. 281 gives a detailed description of the traditional iconography linked to the "Madonna di Loreto", also named "Madonna dei Pellegrini": "A flying house encircled by clouds, the light of the sun and angels upholding the Madonna".

[10] Also defined as agonized, Luigi Moretti, "Discontinuità dello spazio in Caravaggio"

[11] Many of the details of this summary, even if the sources are not cited, belong to Gilles Lambert, *Caravaggio*, Taschen, Kohl 2006 pp. 39-40

[12] The original cited document belongs to Sandro Corradini, *Caravaggio Materiali per un processo*, Alma, Rome 1993 and is referenced in Robb 2001 p. 288.

13 The typically precise Peter Robb writes various pages (in *M the enigma of Caravaggio* pp. 287-298) in which he correctly postulates that the mirrors found in the studio were being professionally used. The author intuits a fundamental link to this device but this notion is not developed and

he almost completely overlooks the camera obscura.

[14] Text attributed to Fiora Bellini, "Tre documenti per Michelangelo da Caravaggio", *Prospettiva*, n. 65 1992 referenced in Robb p. 779.

[15] I first presented this hypothesis in my article "Lo strumento di Caravaggio", Arch'it, March 20, 2007, http://architettura.supereva. com/coffeebreak/20070427/. On the theme of the mirror, I like to reference two madrigals that were brought to my attention by my friend Antonino Di Raimo. One is by Giambattista Marino, "Specchio dell'amata", La Lira, 1602; the other is by Tommaso Stigliani, "Scherzo di Immagini", Canzoniere, 1605. I believe we will eventually uncover an ample resource of songs on the theme of the mirror in the 17th century.

16 Giacomo Della Porta, *Magiae naturalis sive de miraculis rerum naturalium*, 1584 first edition 1558.

[17] David Hockney in *Secret Knowledge* provides a detailed study of the camera obscura and of Caravaggio in pages 49, 54, 110-125, 218-226.

[18] Giulio Mancini, 1617-1621 ca. (additional sources in Robb,2001)

19 Michelangelo Merisi da *Caravaggio*, curated by Mina Gregori, exhibit catalogue at the Roma Palazzo Ruspoli, Electa Milan 1991. One can find a useful summary of the different technical aspects in Debora Bincoletto, "La tecnica di esecuzione di Caravaggio nel periodo romano". http://www.nardinirestauro.it/ dossier_caravaggio/caravaggio_index.htm.

The scholar Roberta Lapucci noted, after the first edition of this book, her own works dedicated to Caravaggio's technique,both traditional (set-up, sketch, color, etc.) as well as optical. One can access some of her articles on the web at http://www.robertalapucci.com/. I reference her article *Caravaggio e l'ottica*, Servizi editoriali, Florence 2005. Lapucci, in her latest writings, proposes the thesis of the painter's use of chemical compounds as aids. These compounds could have allowed him to create a rudimental photographic imprint on the canvas of the projected image.

[20] I am currently researching the physical features of several portraits of Caravaggio's friends as well as his own varied self-portraits that recur often in his works. I am convinced, through this study, that this is a subject often overlooked; albeit noted by Agnes Czobor, "Autoritratti del giovane Caravaggio", *Acta Historiae Artium Academiae Scientiarum Hungaricae*, II, pp. 201-13, Budapest 1955 cited by Maurizio Marine, *Caravaggio. Pictor praestantissimus*, Newton Compton, Rome 2004. I too am convinced that the model of

the "Boy with the basket of fruit" of 1593, (housed at Rome's Galleria Borghese), as well as "Bacchino malato" of a 1594 are both self-portraits of Caravaggio. It is an early work that was in the possession of Cavalier D' Arpino together with the "Bacchino malato" until the seizure of his assets by Scipione Borghese.. The work was painted by a very young Caravaggio and, according some scholars like Mina Gregori, it can be dated prior to 1593. The painter portrays himself in the full bloom of health in the earlier work while the famous "Bacchus malato" was created after a long convalescence from a disease that nearly brought him to his death. If one places the two paintings side-by-side, the likeness of the model is immediately apparent! Comparing the right eye of the two portraits, the marked line of Caravaggio's feature is visibly identical. Both show a matching prominent upper eyelid paired with a barely rendered lower lid and an identical arch of the eyebrow. The rendering of the nose is another characteristic feature of the painter. It is similarly well defined and pointed in both images. The chin and dimple match and similar to the nose appears to tilt upwards. They are clearly of the same person! Viewing the two portraits side-by-side opens up a thousand possibilities that we leave to the reader, but both works could be titled "Self-portrait with Basket of Fruit". Longhi. p.64

[21] Longhi, p.64. Longhi ends this paragraphs with this phrase " But the Caravaggio drew from inner life and without class division, toward simple emotions and even to the restful aspect of objects, of the things of value, in the mirror, to the parity of the men, of the `figure'. "

[22] Regarding the authorship of "Narcissus", originally attributed to Caravaggio by Longhi, and much debated, multiple documents have since been uncovered that confirm Caravaggio as the author (card n. 38 in Maurizio Marini's *Caravaggio. Pictor praestantissimus*). Modernity, in this context, is intended as the revolution of the senses furthered by Impressionism in the second part of the XIX century and asserted again in the first decades of the 19000's with historical vanguards (Cubism, Futurism, and Constructivism). Objectivism of optics, abstraction, the break from the frame and the rejection of the perspective grid make-up some of the basis. The objective of the photographic camera, as well as Galileo's earlier lens, is to some degree the principle player.

[23] The fortunate individual living in Rome can examine any day many of Caravaggio's paintings. They are freely accessible in Churches and various museums. A familiarity with Caravaggio, in my cas , is remote and bu-

ried in my adolescence, similar to key writing ideas that are proposed for publication for the first time even if they have been only been touched upon in two online Arch'it articles of October 2006 and March 2007. My own work on Caravaggio began only after I wrote the essay "Il Motivo di Sant'Ivo" dedicated to Borromini's masterpiece. I believe the essay posited for the first time an iconographic and spatial reading that was coherent and simultaneously overlapping one with the other. I was greatly interested in Peter Robb's M The Enigma of Caravaggio in the early stages of my research. His book offers an insightful reading of Caravaggio's paintings and posits interesting hypotheses on some crucial mysteries in his life. Robb demonstrates that art is not an exclusive prerogative of art historians, whose work though often informative, can be academically insular while art itself is universally accessible. The balance between art and at theory is complicated and can likewise be applied to architecture which in my case, became concretized in my book Giuseppe Terragni Vita e opera, published by Laterza in 1995. After reading Robb, I revisited a good dose of Caravaggio texts. Maurizio Marini's *Caravaggio.Pictor praestantissimus*, Newton Compton Roma 2004 is a very useful and comprehensive theoretical writing on the work. I recommend from the media: "Caravaggio una mostra Impossibile" http://www.caravaggio.rai.it/. This is a very high production by RAI directed by Renato Parascandolo. "Caravaggio's Technique" is a recent video, focusing on the camera obscura, by Whitfield Fine Art also available on YouTube (as well as my own video "Lo strumento di Caravaggio" on YouTube, that examines the painter's self-portraits and portraits of his female friends).

There are many other writings available such as Helen Langdon, *Caravaggio*, Sellerio, Palermo 2001 and Catherine Puglisi, Caravaggio, Phaidon, London 2001. There are numerous exhibition catalogues of which I must mention, once again, Mina Gregori. Michelangelo Merisi da Caravaggio, as well as many other extensions of Caravaggio's influence (Caravaggio e i Giustiniani curated by Silvia Danesi Squarzina, Electa Milan 2001 and Il genio di Roma 1592-1623, curated by Beverly Louise Brown, Rizzoli, Milan 2001) and the recent exhibition catalogue at the Scuderie del Quirinale (Caravaggio, curated by Francesca Cappelletti, Caravaggio e in Caravaggeschi, Il sole 24Ore, Milan 2007. The latter assembles various scholarly studies of recent years but the triad of Longhi, Robb and Marini are my first recommendations for beginning an in-depth research on the subject.

ITool Book Series

Lo Strumento Di Caravaggio /The Instruments of Caravaggio
Roma a-Venire
Quindici Studi Romani
Datemi Una Corda E Costruirò
The IT Revolution Thoughts On A Paradigm Shift
Five Masterworks By Louis Sauer
Urban Voids

Published By Lulu.Com in July 2010
all right reserved

Copy of this book can be bought at

http://stores.lulu.com/ninos

www.ingramcontent.com/pod-product-compliance
Lightning Source LLC
Chambersburg PA
CBHW021940170526
45157CB00005B/2373